Country Music

Published by Smart Apple Media

1980 Lookout Drive, North Mankato, Minnesota 56003

Design and Production by EvansDay Design

Photographs: page 4: Nubar Alexanian/CORBIS;
page 7: JamesLance/CORBIS; pages 8, 11, 25: Bettmann/
CORBIS; page 10: Bradley Smith/CORBIS; page 13: Roger
Ressmeyer/CORBIS; page 14: Lynn Goldsmith/CORBIS;
pages 15, 26, 31: Neal Preston/CORBIS; page 17, 18, 19:
Kevin Fleming/CORBIS; page 21: Underwood &
Underwood/CORBIS; page 23: CORBIS

Library of Congress Cataloging-in-Publication Data

Gish, D. L.

Country music / by D. L. Gish

p. cm. — (World of music)

Includes index.

Summary: Traces the history of country music from its
beginnings through the end of the 20th century, describing
musical instruments, performers, and styles, such as
bluegrass, honky tonk, and country rock.

ISBN 1-58340-020-6

1. Country music—History and criticism—Juvenile literature.
[1. Country music.] I. Title. II. Series: World of music
(North Mankato, Minn.)

ML3524.G57   2002

781.642'09—dc21   99-31749

First Edition

2 4 6 8 9 7 5 3 1

WORLD OF MUSIC

Country Music

D.L. GISH

LASER LIGHTS CIRCLE WHILE THUNDER RUMBLES and lightning flashes overhead. Then comes the rain. As the cool droplets of man-made rain hit their mark, 50,000 heads turn skyward, screaming. But even the roar of the crowd cannot drown out the pounding sound erupting from the towering stack of speakers. That is, not until Garth Brooks steps on stage. Then the crowd and the music become one. Superstars such as Garth Brooks, Reba McEntire, Alan Jackson, and Wynnona Judd made country music one of the hottest-selling sounds by the end of the 20th century. It's hard to imagine that this high-tech, high-energy music was born out of simple instruments played by ordinary people who were just trying to fight off a little loneliness. But that was exactly how it all began.

The area between 16th and 17th Avenues in Nashville, Tennessee, is known as Music Row because of all the studios and recording companies established there.

TWO HUNDRED YEARS AGO, IMMIGRANTS were making their way across North America. Many of the Scottish and Irish settlers, hindered by the Appalachian Mountains, decided to make the foothills of these mountains their home.

Neighbors were scarce in this remote area, so families had to find ways to entertain themselves. Music was one of the few types of entertainment that entire families could participate in. These settlers had traveled many miles over rough terrain, carrying only their most important belongings with them. For many families, one of those items was the fiddle, or violin, an instrument first made popular in England during the 17th century.

Early Scottish- and Irish-Americans enjoyed the fiddle because it could be played to sound sad and mournful or bright and bouncy—much like the bagpipes and harps of their native lands. They also sang ballads of the British Isles as reminders of the friends

Contemporary singer Shania Twain

and families left behind. A ballad uses a chorus of repeated words and phrases to tell an emotional story. The first country music songs were traditional ballads of Ireland and Scotland with new lyrics to tell the stories of daily life in America.

Banjo

The first black performer on the Grand Ole Opry was Deford Bailey, born in Tennessee in 1899. The first black to win a Grammy award for country music was Charlie Pride.

COUNTRY MUSIC CONTINUED TO CHANGE as people of different cultural backgrounds worked their way across America, bringing their musical traditions and instruments with them. The blues, especially, had a great influence on early country music. Groups of slaves working in fields in the South sang about their lives, combining different rhythms or beats at the same time. Traditionally, blues were sung to raise spirits and sometimes to send secret messages. Along with the blues came the introduction of the "banjar," or banjo, one of the most important instruments in country music.

The banjo is a string instrument of African origin that arrived in North America with the slave trade. It started out as an animal hoof or gourd, then later evolved into a wooden hoop, with four pieces of animal gut stretched tightly for the strings that were plucked. In the 1830s, a man named Joel Sweeney added a fifth string to the banjo, which gave it a range of sound similar to that of the fiddle.

In the early part of their career in the 1930s, the Carter Family traveled with Leslie Riddles, a black man whose only job was to memorize the melodies of traditional mountain music shared by local citizens.

With the introduction of trains in the mid-1800s, many rural people were able to get away from their daily routines and see how others lived. This is one way country music spread across the United States. People heard others using the same instruments but in a different manner, then took those new ideas home and continued to reshape their own musical traditions.

JOHNNY CASH AND
TAMMY WYNETTE

THE FIRST
Recordings

Married at the age of 13 and a mother of four children by the age of 18, Loretta Lynn went on to record and perform many songs about her early life as a coal miner's daughter.

COUNTRY MUSIC SPREAD RAPIDLY AFTER World War I, due to the rising popularity of records and phonographs. The sound city dwellers referred to as "hillbilly" music (because it came from the mountain regions of the South) soon crisscrossed America.

The first country musicians to make a record were Texas fiddlers Eck Robertson and Henry Gilliland. On June 30, 1922, they went to Victor Records in New York and asked to make a recording. Initially denied, they persisted . . . and persisted. So, simply to get them out of the office, the Victor engineer agreed to help them record some duets and solos.

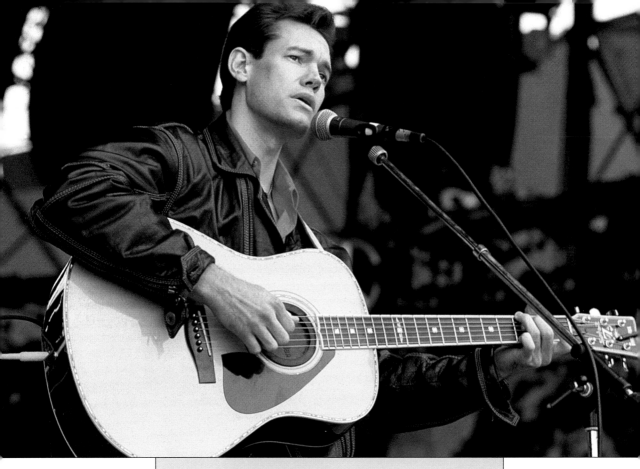

At first, the recording just sat on a shelf at Victor Records. When the company's sales started to fall off with the arrival of radio, the owners decided to look for some new music. The first thing Victor Records did was release Robertson and Gilliland's fiddling songs—and to their surprise, the public bought them as fast as they were produced. Victor Records and other music companies decided to scour the South for more music of that type.

Kitty Wells sang backup for her husband, Johnnie Wright, until he encouraged her to perform on her own. This shy young woman would go on to become known as the "Queen of Country Music."

A Victor Records executive, Ralph Peer, spent two weeks in July 1927 in a small town on the Virginia-Tennessee border recording musicians who had come from all over the South. Two of those acts recorded songs that would have a big impact on the future of country music: Jimmie Rodgers and the Carter Family.

COMEDIAN
MINNIE PEARL

on Stage

For more than 30 years, Grandpa Jones and Minnie Pearl showcased their comedy routines on the Grand Ole Opry and other live stage shows.

CONSISTING OF A.P., SARA, COUSIN Maybelle, and several others, the Carter Family came from Virginia and recorded many of the old Appalachian Mountain songs they had been performing throughout the South. Their music best demonstrated the way country blended voices and instruments into its own unique sound.

The other artist who made an important recording was Jimmie Rodgers. Making music was not Rodgers's first career. He had been a train brakeman in the South and Southwest. Then, at the age of 28, he had to retire from the railroad after developing

tuberculosis. After that, he took his guitar and began singing country music songs about life on the railroad.

Records continued to sell, but it was radio that eventually became the most popular outlet for country music. Radio stations started to broadcast shows that entertained families in remote areas of the country as well as those in big cities. The first of these live shows was the Grand Ole Opry, which began broadcasting in 1925 on the radio station WSM. The show held live perform-

A BLUEGRASS BAND
PERFORMING ONSTAGE

ances on Friday and Saturday nights in the Ryman Auditorium, a converted church in Nashville, Tennessee.

At first, the Grand Ole Opry was a way for part-time musicians to promote their live appearances elsewhere, but it has since become a career-making venue for country music artists.

Roy Acuff and the Smoky Mountain Boys be-came regulars on the Grand Ole Opry show in 1938. Through the years, Acuff worked hard to promote the Grand Ole Opry and remained active in recording and performing until his death in 1992.

Hank Williams, Sr., could not read or write music, but he became one of the most popular country music stars in history. He learned to play guitar with the help of a black Alabama street singer named Rufe Payne. Hank Williams died in 1953 at the age of 29.

IN THE LATE 1930S, MOVIES BECAME A favorite American pastime. Westerns were especially popular, which in turn made cowboy music popular. Movie cowboys roaming the ranges of the West came from diverse cultures. Appalachian music, blues, Mexican waltzes, and church hymns all came together to influence the music of the Western movies, and country music soon became known as country-western music.

Performers such as Roy Rogers and Gene Autry, the "Singing Cowboy," also helped to introduce the harmonica and guitar to country music. The harmonica was popular with

HANK WILLIAMS, SR.

the cowboys because it was small and fit easily in a pocket or saddle bag. Like the fiddle, the harmonica could be played to sound either happy or sad.

In the movies, the guitar was always a cowboy's instrument of choice. In real life, however, because of its high cost, the guitar didn't make its way to rural America until the early to mid-1900s. The mandolin—a small, guitar-like instrument—was also a favorite instrument of the singing cowboys.

Another instrument closely identified with country-western music is the steel

In 1987, George Strait's hit Ocean Front Property *was the first country album to enter the charts at number one.*

pedal guitar, which uses electronic devices and pedals to sustain the notes. The steel pedal guitar became an important part of the western swing sound, a blend of Texas fiddle music and jazz—one of many variations growing out of country-western music.

HANK WILLIAMS, JR.

Barbara Mandrell and the Mandrell Sisters *was a popular country music variety show on television from 1980 to 1982.*

BY THE 1940S, COUNTRY MUSIC WAS changing again. This time it took two very different paths. One new form was bluegrass music, which originated in the Appalachian Mountains. Bluegrass usually consisted of five or six musicians playing stringed instruments such as the banjo, mandolin, fiddle, and bass. Many bluegrass singers were known for their high-pitched, soulful voices.

Bill Monroe, considered the father of bluegrass music, made his first recordings in 1936. With his band, the Blue Grass Boys, Monroe put on a show complete with musicians, comedians, and dancers.

Bluegrass music continued to be a popular part of the country sound up through
the 1960s. It eventually became the alterna-
tive music of choice for city dwellers who
were tired of the hard-pounding rock and
roll sound.

While some country fans were listening to
bluegrass music, others were enjoying
honky tonk. The term "honky tonk" ap-
pears to have originated in Oklahoma in
1891 when *The Daily Ardmorite* reported that
"the honk-a-tonk last night was well att-
ended by ball-heads, bachelors and leading
citizens." This odd phrase made its way into

country music in 1936, when a musician by the name of Al Dexter recorded a song called "The Honky Tonk Blues." The phrase soon became associated with the lively dance halls that were established up and down the highways of the Southwest.

Perhaps the greatest honky tonk singer of all time was Hank Williams, Sr. Born in Alabama in 1923, Hank Williams sang upbeat songs of good times, paydays, dancing, and celebrating—as well as sad ballads about lost wages and abandoned families. Williams gave honky tonk music its trademark: the celebration and sorrow of life.

In 1970, country-rock singer Tanya Tucker had her first hit at the age of 12 with the song "Delta Dawn."

DURING THE LATE 1950S, COUNTRY music seemed to lose sight of its traditional roots. Many money-hungry record producers told songwriters what to write and performers what to sing. To some, tradition meant nothing compared to sales. Country artists began to use orchestras and background vocals during this time. By the 1960s, this chart-crossing music became known as the Nashville Sound or "countrypolitan." The goal of performers such as Patsy Cline, Jim Reeves, Eddie Arnold, and the Statler Brothers was to record music that would reach a broader audience.

Then, by the 1970s, country music started to move away from Nashville. New sounds were established in such cities as Bakersfield, California, and Austin, Texas. Performers started taking control of their own music, too. More amplified instruments were used, and the country sound was blended with southern rock music to create what became known as country-rock or outlaw country music. Performers making it to the top of the charts included Johnny Cash, Merle Haggard, Willie Nelson, Waylon Jennings, and the group Alabama. Fans of rock and roll were drawn to these new sounds in country music, putting country songs on pop record charts for the first time since the 1950s.

Reaching popularity performing outlaw music, singer-songwriter Willie Nelson helped organize Farm Aid concerts in 1985, 1986, and 1987. These were events that helped raise millions of dollars for American farmers.

In 1990, Garth Brooks sold out an 18,000-seat arena in just 37 minutes, breaking the record held by rocker Bruce Springsteen.

WHEN THE POPULARITY OF CROSSOVER music began to fade by the late '80s, a new group of Nashville-based performers came onto the scene. They called themselves "new traditionalists," and it was their goal to return country music to its roots. While the electric guitars of country-rock remained, new emphasis was put on the sounds of the fiddle, mandolin, banjo, and steel pedal guitar. Some of the performers that grew in popularity with this refreshing sound were the mother-daughter duo the Judds, as well as George Strait and Randy Travis.

Today, country music comes in all forms and is heard all over the world. Artists such as The Dixie Chicks and Brad Paisley stay close to traditional country sounds, while Jo Dee Messina and LeAnn Rhimes have found success remaking old country and rock favorites. Other artists such as Shania Twain and Faith Hill continue to top both the country and pop charts with their crossover hits. It's anyone's guess what lies in the future for country music, but one thing is certain: country music is still the music of rural America—of working people living life one day at a time.